THE BUZZARD AND THE PEACOCK

THE
BUZZARD
AND
THE
PEACOCK

POEMS BY NED O'GORMAN

Harcourt, Brace & World, Inc.
New York

© *1961, 1962, 1964 by Ned O'Gorman*

First edition

Library of Congress Catalog Card Number: 64-11527

Printed in the United States of America

Some of the poems in this volume previously appeared in *Commonweal, Pax,* and *Poetry.*

To Valborg Anderson, Dorothy Van Ghent,
and Roger L. Stevens

CONTENTS

THE BUZZARD AND THE PEACOCK

THREE EXPLANATIONS
IN A TIME OF DARKNESS
WHEN THE MIND AND HEART AND WILL
WERE SEEN TO BE DIVIDED
FROM THE SELF

Wethersfield House—Summer, 1962

1. The Stone Lions

Each lion a thought. My mind
tripped up on its own relevance.
I turn to the valley, the sounds
of children and the angelus. A
rabbit runs upon his green fancy.
Each lion a thought. (How dark
my dark blood, how rank my heart.)
The narrow forms that hold my
brain in place eye the stone lions
in their stone lions' face. Each
lion a thought and in the strata
of their hearts marble and quartz
move upon the jungle and their claws
pace ferrous brush, through plate-glass
mists and oxide grasses. The nether
lion grapples the pebbles at his feet
and leads the field mouse and the beaver
like sticks into the jaws of his
intent. The one roaming the zenith

spits dews of lamentation and
knocks the hummingbird from the folly
of sweet. In the glory of their
world I fall in arcs of magnanimity
to this straitening and dementia of sense.

The lions crouch, as this summer
crouches, upon mind, nerve and valley.
I see them mount the sands and
parapets to howl near the fires
and nail the impala to the dust.
Their blazons, their bodies, their
cold minds, my crystalline heart
stalk each other through torpid
centuries of the wild—winged, agile
aboriginal and a liquor of supreme
grace bursts from the light.

2. *The Toad with the Blind Eye*

Often the mind, having no use
for joy spoils in its deliberate
fear and holds all brightness
high, beyond the reach of will
and nerve. To find its balance,
where it can ride free of sound
and sensibility, the mind will
treat the demons to a feast of
spirit and after the long devouring
visitation will lean on its

advantage and be dull and dream,
toss all sweetness and scrape
the barren forms of fear.
These days have been a loss
and a habitation of fear.
I dreamed a friend had died and
for a year I wept in that boundless
grief of sleep: one night I held
a hive of evil languors to my
chest and woke to harbor anguish
all the day. It is a dementia of
my sight, this slow biting silence
of this summer grief. But such
dementia is a cracking of
vision:
to see within that which is
common usage must always defer
to new ritual. It is the highest
flowering of my highest good.

In the pool, at the bottom of
fieldstone steps near a grove
where a green and bronze naiad
rubs the light, a toad, the size
of a strong man's hand flayed out,
sits and twitches one blind eye.
When I dove naked in the pool at
sunrise I felt his crippled foot
and blind eye shut out the speed and
cool labors of my blood and burn about
my ankle a bright green ring of weed.

3. The Buzzard and the Peacock

If the mind could build its own paysage
it would live in storm
and typhoon where there
was always wind.

But beloved by none other than itself
the mind asserts its singular
grace and elects to live
in a land of

stillness and perfect vantages and cold valleys.
It makes the heavens and the
broad plain the holds and
frames of sense.

On this resplendent pinnacle of fear
the way to the center is a
gnome's trick not the
strategy of man.

It is difficult, but given the correspondence
of the day, the stars and the spirit
it is perhaps possible to
find a sign

in nature to define it. The buzzard
and the peacock on a summer day
explained in the style and excess
of their flights

the quest the lions urged upon my thought.
The buzzard is the will; the mind,
the peacock. Peacock-Mind
trailing his

divertimento on the lawn, bearing in
his tail the weightless
tendrils of splendor
and conception.

Buzzard-Will, plumed for carnage, flies
straight up to the winds,
seeks out new blood
and finds one day,

strutting on the shadow of his hen,
Peacock-Mind and eying her
like lion meat,
swoops

with plumes ploughing the wind.
Blazons flame in the
marigolds. But sure
as death

one night, Peacock-Mind, in her slow
sortie to the peak of
the roof will knock
down Buzzard-

Will, gorged to the chin with his
hen, to the court where
on triangles and squares
he'll bite the night.

ANIMAL-LIFE

He covered his eyes
and fell to his knees
when he thought he had seen
what the hyena sees.

He took to the hills
and built a new shack
when he dreamed he had died
with a claw in his back.

One night he saw crawling
under the door
a form like a trumpet
and called for the Lord.

A lion had strayed from
his lair in the rocks—
when he heard it roar
he doubled the locks.

He put up barbed wire
and filled in the cracks,
and walked with his eyes
cast down to find tracks

of beasts that he knew
and those that he didn't.
Animal-Life, the eyes
of the beetle, the sibilant

smirk of the toad brought
tremors and fits to the brain.
And in his connections with
life as he feared it came

neck of the vulture,
beasts from the water,
the horn of the rhino,
the dirge of the slaughter;

and he trained and he fasted
and hardened his waist
for the bestial encounter
he knew was his fate.

His shoulders grew broad,
his belly went flat
he supped on wild nuts
and ran off the fat.

He studied the stars, saw signs
of the hunter, drew in his breath,
put salt on his tail, and when he was
certain, whistled for death

and strode in his boots to
the prairie. The sky was blue
the grasses were green
and high in the sky flew

the sun like a gullet and a
bird with the face of a ghoul.
He heard feet on the sand,
felt a tongue on his neck, a pool

of still water churned dark
at the center; in the brush
flashed a horn, but nothing was there
no fang and no claw, just the hush

of their tails as the farm beasts
strolled by and a thin white
shadow that followed him home
where he slept in his boots, set a light

on the gate and whistled for death.
His belly went soft;
wild flowers grew on the roof;
his eyes went dull and a frost

slid down on the light. In the
sharp winds above him hovered lower
and lower each day and each night
the white bird hovered lower

from the ridge of the roof,
to the fence, to the sill,
to the top of his head. When
it had eaten into his brain, till

eyes of the hunter met the
eyes of the bird
he smelt in his mouth, when his soul went wild
the pelt of the viper, the hoofs of the herd.

VEGETABLE-LIFE

Where the pulp lifts its germ and the sludge of beauty
                                                  sighs,
where the leaf pulls the branch to the breathy earth,
where the rind cracks and the buds rust into petals,
where the clove steams and the cinnamon bark spits out
                                          cinnamon air,
where roots sweat and the earth boils in curds of steaming
                                                  mud,
where the stem draws up the seed and holds it like a lamb
                                          to the sun,
where flowers rest their animal heads,
there, full throated, limp with seed, lush and smiling is
Vegetable-Life.

To come upon her you must journey through the rains,
and sleep through a night of fish smells;
there must be a dead man in a hot room,
there must be a basket of figs and plums on the pier,
there must be no new ship in the harbor,
there must be the sound of flowers falling upon flowers,
there must be no children swimming in the salt pools.

Where the Flamboyant spills into the vulcan dust,
where the wild pig chews up the door frames,
where the leper kneads his bones,
where the sun is stuffed with guns,
where the water flows like honey from the tap,
where black flies swell in the gekko's translucent belly,

where these are, there is
Vegetable-Life: The Sultana of the Vine,
The Goddess of the Harvest Gone Bad, The Spectrum
                                        Swallower.

In an ointment of wild saps, ripe fronds and mosses, tumid
                                        wheat
and barley, Abundance pours down over the head, heavy
                                        with pollen
and in the puce interrogation of the harvest
the intellect sprouts leaves.

THE HAWK-KITE FALLING

Tissue of air that held the bird,
the black hawk-kite rent.

The light that shaped the tissue
of air the black kite rent,

flying in this fractious heat,
entered and undid the springs

within it and tissue of air tore
and crackled in an elephantine

cackle and the hawk-kite fell
with a cry that came from the edge

of prey, shrieking to the corners
of my mind and the gasping sands.

Sound of the bird that fell from
the tissue of air the hawk-kite rent,

butchered its way through the percussions
of these pharaonic ethers and in its

clammering defile I saw the hawk-kite
stop and separate, claw and plumage,

like the crux of a mechanical saw torn away
by an ebony bole; a spinning screw maimed

on a coral ridge; the threads and frame of
a loom snapped at the point of sheerest tension;

a man gone mad atop a pillar who falls
and scrapes the air with damned embraces.

And held together by the light, the tissue
of air and the yell of the bird, the kite

came to a stone and livid stop before my eyes
and in a fit of plunder took me for his

carrion. Plunging toward the groaning
earth, my body rolled in his feathers,

at the last millimeter before we shattered
and swallowed the dry wind, a measure of grace

no larger than a fly cast its shadow on the
land and held us in peerless equilibrium.

A sweet wind rushed under us and the
black kite rent from the dilemma of

his questing form regained his shape,
sable and sage as an arrow and flew

to the climax of the hour. I felt within
me grow a granite, black and floating power.

A CHILD OF LIGHT, A CHILD OF DARK

One day he knuckled under and they found
him in the garden, a stick in his hand,
dead, watching the world, rigor by rigor,
stop before his eyes. The gardener
covered him with straw, called the women,
who washed him, stuffed his nose with
cotton and bound him to a board with linen
bands. His father took the black mare
and hunted until dark. His brothers
wept in the trees and in the morning
they covered him with flowers and spade
by spade his body jammed tight into
the hillside. The world was maimed.
Its brooding permanence forgot, it bolted
to the tip of everlastingness.

(Each man who finds his way in from the void
is a child of darkness or a child of light;
the harbinger or devourer of light.)

A queerness touched the six years that
he lived. He spoke with darkness and
from the badlands of his dreams told tales
of the fusion and destruction of spheres.
He could not bear the subtle hours and hid
in the dark halls until the night had
filled the spaces he despised. He railed
at mirrors with a stick and filled

clay jugs with water from a forest stream
and bore the sun he caught to all the
animals and flowers in the gardens.

I saw this dead child's face brought to
me by his kin, young Paolo, sixty years
from the year he died. The painting,
hidden in the attic of a country house
for fear of what he seemed to be, was
this child's face, but Paolo, braced by the
free passions of his strident seed, flourished
in the secret ordinance of man and etched
out the harvest of the dead boy's ruined joy.
He is no instrument of demons; dreams
but tells no tales. Though what he sees may be
the ultimate declensions of his sense he bears
it like a stone at the crucial stress of an arch
bears in its thick spatial tact the beauty
of the span, the entrance light, the brigand in the apse.

I HAD A TEARING SCRAPE WITH CRIME

I had a tearing scrape with crime
in a farmhouse of tall clocks,
chairs with legs of lion paws,
heavy doors, stone ovens and
white stone lintels. Through
the deep windows the sun bore
into the roses and apples of the
wainscot. I feasted on the
blood and stone of the black joys.
Once when the spirit flew the
catwalks of the spheres I took
an ax into the fields and cut
the wild rose hedges back and
burned the boughs on a hill where
pheasants flew past the spiraling
thorns. Somewhere in the fields,
among the warm rocks, a magnet stone,
fallen from the marrow of the
skies, lay among the first fruits
of the lolling world. The fire
died, the sap drained from the
twigs and the scorched ax lay white
as boiling milk in the dark. The
black, grey, yellow, red birds
flew to the lowest branches of the
oaks. I drove the ax into
the hill and from the earth spilt

the ages of bronze, iron and gold
as if the roots and minerals of the
world had been gored and seeded by a prism.

THREE AFRICAN POEMS FOR
THE CHILDREN SHRADY

1. *The Rhino Dreams*

The rhino dreamed a barge with riggings of grass
driven by an alabaster wind: woke to find
the day in a convulsive ebb. He dreamed
a plain of craters and snows that moved in voids
of braying gasses. A season scratched his pelt.
He dreamed a joining of parts but once perceived
the idea stopped to rot within him in a lake
of feathers. He smells the carbons and ash
of the grave and wakes to find he slept all night
in the deluge of the beast he killed, who hangs
head down in the craggy temple of his gut.
One night he dreamed he grew black wings and was
reborn and woke to find a mailed hand on his
heart, his spine awry, an ax upon his horn.

2. *The Rhino Awakes*

The black cipher keeps its own council in the field: as ore
in weeds: as the captain the angle of the sumptuous guns.

In the middle distance, from the hollow between two hills
comes a ruffle of power: at the ear of the rhino knocks a
                                                    sound:

an egret sleeps upon his brow: from the base of the skull
to the heart, to the imponderable knot of spleen,

particle and continuity of his mass unwind and into the
                                                    black
increase of sleep sifts the crags and spumes of the Kingdom.

Parasites creak down rills of nerves and with a great
heaving of all the soul, it is in space. There

is a universal disfigurement of all objects; the world
like a molten loaf of density is hooked by the beast,

double-horned: the eruption of leviathan, hobbled:
it was as if a blind rut screeched.

3.   The Rhino Stands Still in a Field of Lilies

His eyes
two points
of damage
in the
breast of
a cut
down giant:
his legs
four axies
of planet
Mars: his
neck the

barrel of
a still
cannon: his
ears two
gates of
Tophet: his
belly is
a drum
of lead
over a
drum of
copper over
a drum
of black
bone: his
paws: four
bolts: his
mouth the
slit back
of a
scarab: the
rhino stands
still as
a balanced
rock over
a wedding
march: as
a deaf
nun on
a cymbal.

The difference
between man
and rhino
is that
when the
lilies moved
on their
stems I
looked down
and it
did not:
when the
black crane
cooed on
the pitch
of the
snow face
I covered
my eyes
and picked
up a
stone: it
did not.

COUNSELS TO A BENEDICTINE NOVICE

1. The Deception of Fullness

Be it this or that tense or fine
brick walled garden, the herbs
hoed and linked into bitter tracks.
Be it the brute sun on the copper
tower or the trout flexing in
the stream or the tousled fox,
deafened, sliding through the brush.
Be it the quail beaten from the wheat
building pillars in the air
to hide his ascension from the net.
Be it the rose like a rude stylities
on its stem or the light rustling in
the armor of night. Be it the heart
logged with keening or the mind
stuck on the pike of its responsibility,
summer is a doubtful vengeance
on the snows and will not hold.

2. The Deception of Decrease

It is brave to flee decrease,
to prick the lean pretense
and burn the barren stalk.

It is a quarry to hawk
hidden in a blind, backward
to the center, away from the lair

in no abandonment to encounter.
Learn this law: it is to be
shunned. Hold a mirror

to the sterile drone. Be
the yellow-spined nun and hide
like a seed in your linen ark.

3. The Deception of Death

The great-gun icicle is tilted
    in the sun. It will find
you out at the expanse where
    hitched to the neck of
the word, self turns, belled
    like a cat on the rim
of God. Enormous levers of snow
    flick mountains through
hollows of black ice. In fairest
    seasons the heart will
tend toward zero. Be defunct.
    Warm yourself, capitulate to the
blaze; await the sun.

4. *Spring*

This is the climate of perfection
and will not decrease
except as things
decrease
that live

so entirely that the flourishing
rebounds, one beauty
and another beauty
fully
without necessity

as things that branch and lower
into loveliness
point on point
of light,
refulgent,

without end. It is Christ that's the season.
As the earth rides
Christ draws in
the reins
taut;

bands together hawks and robins,
daffodils and streams
as the sun rolls in
winged and
praised

by Christ, Primavera's plant bannered
and blazoned. Christ
rides the hills
where snails
prod

light from the buckling dirt
and the plow lurches
stirred to cut.
The furrow
and the sun

shine triumphant in a corinthian harvest.

A RECTIFICATION OF THE LYRIC

I know they say it is music;
that it is music we find
in this word we have sought
and carried to the poem.
I know it is song; they
have said it is; time
and the fault of time
is the lyric moat we build
around rime. I have
learned it and to unlearn
it takes my spirit and my
flesh from one field of
darkness to another. Music
once learned is like love
once learned, ultimate
and untranslatable. Now
the other side of music
turns its face toward me,
tipping base and treble clef
onto the rigid void and
facing into my heart the
coin of light that in
seraphic furnaces had forged
a circle, ardent and packed
with the runes and hammered
emblems of the sun. So light
comes upon me in a second
tactic. The first was the crack

to the brain when music
pulling a wagon of light lifted
up its marauding foot
and struck my face with sound.
Learn then it is light
we seek. Not music but music's
interior places. Light. Neither
the aerial light nor the light
that rests upon stone and spring
flowers; not light of the sun
or the autumn garden but light
in the cruse of tile that
moves behind the cliff. Within
the greyhound's pelt. The light
that spoils in the torpid
stone hovering like myrrh
in the quarry's bin.
It is light we seek. Light
at light's midpoint. The mute
light at the dull center
of sound. Light. The bud,
the phrase, the climax.
Exemplum: Yeats, Catullus;
passion and myth cross by
music into light. Or, music
attaches to light like a drum-
stick to the hide of the
kettle. Or, a finger moving
down across water. Like a grove
of birch tempered by sun
into a relief of static fire.

Light has no modality,
no dictum of pleasure.
Light rules now
and rules the poem and music
on its animal of prism
comes blazing down. . . .

"The soul must seek light
by following light; though
it has no place and its
brightness casts a shadow
on this light, less bright
but dazzling nevertheless."

We turn on our heels and
undo the cords and locks that
have held us down and set
aside our children and our books;
burn down our ships;
cast our lines out into the sea
the sea where there is an
unsettling on the waters—
something moves beneath
and shows its eye now and then
above the surface; there
is light above us, beneath
us, at our wrists, over our
feet, light nips at the edge
of the sea; noisesome as
wild geese fish push one against
the other to tunnel into

the trembling reef. There is
nothing left at all, anywhere.
Place has ceased to be; all
herbs are crushed together;
time is broken in the corner
of the eye. Only two things
remain: the circle in space
where the earth had been—
a bright dent on the light—
and over the whole vault
held by the thing it is,
a coil of brightness spells
trumpet alpha and flame omega.

TWO HOLY INCIDENTS

1. God's First Name

He washed the dirt from his hands, stripped,
stood beneath the waterfall, climbed
the rocks above and lay upon the hot stones,
stretching into the streams of light
that pulled their tight waters of flowers
and wild birds across the forest. Girded
with a breechclout woven by the hands of
many girls he walked across the river at
the foot of the waterfall and with the ease
of twigs and rose hedges strode through
the wilderness to an altar atop a hill,
its central pedestal tied into the ground
by cords and girders of roots and mica bolts.
From the hill there were steeples, dove cotes,
voices in the barley fields, bells, and
in the distance through the brain flew
two winged, black birds. Upon the altar
he placed avocados, lemons, blackberries,
apples and a coronal cluster of grape; he
surrounded them with wood and at the right
incidence of the sun, when the black birds were
at the crest of their black flight he set
fire to the fruits and vegetables and God's
first name arose. He was called: burning
fruit; burning vegetables; food of black birds.

2. *Bantam Cock*

The hens, splashing in their heat,
hie to his lusty promenade. The
widows feel thunder in their claws;
across their blood comes the
cackle of virtue, clicking in the
vermilion plumes that set ablaze
the holy oils. In the unmixed

dazzle of space black birds draw
honey from the brain and out
of the night, from the sleeping barn,
stalks the bantam cock, his belly
and throat sirens in the hens' deaf
wombs. Men and boys, asleep in
towers and caves, wake, and come to

watch his feathered durance coil
through the brood. The leaping
sperm prods the womb; in the warm
hollows of the night a cry of joy
springs from the steeples and
barley fields. And the dawn flashes
wanton on its burning pole.

THE SEA—EAST HAMPTON

1.

Like a spliced melon
the sea lay knocked open
at his feet. Or he
had knocked it open with
running on its edge,
tumbling the seeds,
doing leaps and
dives on the surfaces—

a scroll of flaming parchment
flinging back onto its
center pin. Or he read it
open, stamping the margin,
distending the vocables
of Poseidon so they
cracked like a cock
swallowing the sun.

Reeled in, the sea
constructs nerves of
light like cat-gut on
the mind and takes
the thrust of driven thoughts
building tumuli of
winds and the winds' hot stuffs
of kelp and ambergris.

A dog-fish, a sting ray
and a blue crab, at
swells and chords of din,
lay fractured on the
searing strand in
boiling rot. The dog-fish
inverse mouth agape; the ray
tooled by flies;

the blue crab sprawled
on the moving sands
sinking into the charged
foundation. He saw
corruption swing on
the tidal lights and
the shifting polar reef
slid beneath his heel

and the lily sea, the grazing
sea, the bitch-wet, bent
on the forged elements and
locked lips on the source
draining the slut wild
to a dry web of air
sucking light like a
whipped shark to the bottom.

2.

He thought he had been born before this birth
in the sea, the child of two water sprites
who mated on a glide of light, near a firth
of coral brush and opaque golden dunes,
their bodies struck in the tow of the lusting
tides where sea-crystal flashed and sea-flares
fell on the eddies and contradictions of the
southerly currents. There, in the angling
of love they drew out his soul from the seed
and generation of the waters, lying on the
charging air like two birds on a glacial mass
pulling a prey of wild fish through lean
and shuttered lights. And when his body burst
its traps and stood graced in knells leviathan,
soul broke through scales and braids of oil
and sailed entranced upon a grazing sea.

3.

Ahead of us a white light made from the
fume and friction of the sea rose at the place
the waves splayed out onto the sand. Mounted
high on the back of the galloping waters the
sea moved toward land where some memory stirred
its blood and sought out the rivers, the streams,
the pools, the waterfalls that gather in their
hides and husks the stasis and tissue
of the sea. This white smoke, this bodied

water, arched its back, and took to the dunes,
girded with the hot ores and sizzling hydrogen
of the tides. When it looked up out over the
line that draws the world into a sphere I felt
the forged images of tidal trumpets and
the keels of embossed and scalloped barges pulling our blood through the battering wild. And
like an eye seeking out the light from a star
that fell in some malediction's flux, the sea
sought out the mountain lake that held a giant
vein of salt like a sliver of seed at the dayspring.

THE HERETIC AND THE DANCER

1.

He thought God open; laid out
his brain before him; cut the stout
muscle of his thigh apart; held back
his mouth and pierced through the black
den of his throat to his neck
and skewered him to a table, the wreck
of his ambitions. He stared him down,
his mind aloft in the anatomy of God
where the mystery of the veins, their brown
and copper lights break on his mind like a sod
lifted high into the air where the fork
rings and the pikes pull the sun
into the laggard marrow in the shaft. "I'd talk
in images of farmer and clown, of the dumb

butcher and the simple weavers of bright
colored flags and mats, but the tight
wit and riddle in the mind keep God
locked to the table and the rod
and plier of my trade grind God open
and I fall, thrust by the molten
signs of his bowels, to my saw where devils
gather; where I speak of spirits and
dry theophanies. The revels
of my anatomy go by and God lies, brand
and iron of my mind cooling in the shade,

upon my table, where his eyes blaze
with wonder that his skull once so grave
and lean is broken, amazed

and disassembled: O Lord rejoin again
together wit and passion that strain
in the tow of your olympian blood; no place
but woman and flower lament and die; black grace
frets my thoughts and I am become the pyre
of my mind; brow crackles and smoke and fire
reach to my brain's cloven blue
where I rig slaughter and split your marrow bone.
The moon and sun fill my eyes with two
burning discs; beneath my hammer, stone
planes and ruby metal chip and spark. Lord
bind me to your broken center, for my knife
moves in the last strokes of my anatomy toward
your heart where my heart hovers in its little life."

2.

Hurt by one indiscretion, she fell.
And between the edge of life and the edge
of the toothed fires, by an effort
of her back, she leaned on the force that
drew her onto the hot jaws and held there—
while the shades roared
extinction.

Earth electricity forced the light
and the world glowed in the spoil of her stance.
Crocus and wild rose, vines that bear
white flowers and red berries surged up
at her feet as if she'd been touched by aged
and scarred dynamos and currents.
Stars, suns, moons and comets, spheres and
galaxies lurched back upon the void
when the dancer stamped her heel on the sizzling turf.

HUNTING HAWKS IN ETHIOPIA

On a scarp, two mile high, the arrows
lie side by side in the quiver. Narrow
yellow trees and black pillars lay
on the dawn and on such a plain day
I set out to hunt for hawks. Believe it,
it was my wish to trace a leaf, pit
my dogs at the quarry, walk on to the lake,
but it was a plain day and the great
hawks come down from their cold wills.
Mice fall from their claws; they kill
all rest; hawks are everywhere. In stone bowls
of fire two mock suns hang from poles
of cedar to pull the hawks to earth, run
vulcan in the long waste of the hunt. I drum
the leather quiver and sit awaiting hawks on this plain day.

The air spoils. The sun burns on and I wait
upon the hawks. My dogs sleep and I plait
a net of thorn; my boots kindle. The sun shines
on the high winds and when I tire of repose I line
my sights toward the air above me
to seek the killer I will kill. A bee
on a scalloped band of sound pulls
on my wrist and the hawks, on lulls
of tempest, come down from their cold wills on this plain
                                                            day.

I walk out into the roaring field. The stone
bowls upturn in the dust and a green bone
of power drives through my peace. Hawks turn
like dice in the tumbling lights as I learn
the law and mercy of the hawk that I will kill on this plain
                                                      day.

I saw a wild clawing in the air and took
my bow and seized an arrow. A hook
of black pierced the sun and I let
the arrow fly. Hawks everywhere. A net
of black feathers buried deep the light
and at my feet the bird lay dead: bright
the hawk's eyes; bright his plumage
and upon my heart a damaged glory lay and homage
to the wild bird's blood my still blood paid
and I put down my weapons in the night of this plain day.

CORN, WINE AND OIL

1. Corn

The late bird of prey counts out his harvest.
The frost links the field mouse in its crystal
treachery. A driven heat is upon the burrows.
Corn stalks bring down their silken hammers
on the land. In the pitch fandangle of the
willow the pheasants braid their plumage
in the wind. The fields move out upon the
night lifting high their pollened, lusty poles
like green summer gods. Gold kernels clamp
upon the husk. On the hills and in the valleys
the men hear the noise of the waterwheel turning
the millstone; sacks and barrels fill up with
grain and light, pollened, silken and of the tinct
of gold tips through the bins its immaculate fire.

The loaf swells in the oven. The leaven cracks
and yellow bread stands open in the white stone
kitchen. (I would so knead, pummel and break the
seeds of my ambition that each single angle and
occurrence of my wit—sheaves of wheat, wooden
carts, the implements of husbandry, stallions and
fish—would glow in the bright excursions of the
winnowing staffs.) The radiant cipher of the
loaf, common as brick, keen as a leaf, stands
like the wide sun, steaming, on the sill.

2. Wine

i.

The grape swims in its bright reliquary
as no spinnaker ever swam in the windy
sun and though it has scriptural and nodal
lineage and names it grows best in warm
climates where each year the seasons bring
rain and frost in degrees of unequal
ardor and twist the vineyards to the ground
or strike them barren with the hail that
tips from the sun. At a settling of gold
and mercury red wings stir the light
and the world is blown scarlet and the syrups
and philters in the air cut under the root
and push through heat and mud the grape
onto the hot flank of the branch. The mind,
flushed like a kite brushing the edge of
a comet, moves down upon its roots, salt
on its tail, sharp for the kill.

ii.

Thought, said the lions, is the space
the herons see between their image
in the water
and our bite.

Thought, said the hedgehogs, is the space
from the catamount's clubbed
paw to the pistons
of our umber spikes.

Thought, said the phoenix,
is the space between my
eyelash burning
and the flaring sod.

Thought, said the eagles, is the space
between the corded eddies
of the light and
our shimmering fall.

Thought, said the giraffe, is the space
between the steeple of my
body and the belled
shuttles in the air.

Thought, said man, is the space
between my whip and
the bestial skirmish
on the deserts

and upon the hills where the animals
turning on their marauding wills
gather to rejoice. Dizzy, embracing,
howling they turn off into the hollows

of their dark, piped by the nightingales
who sing in the dark veins of the vineyard
and the world's delivered up to the harvest,
the animals and the harvesters.

3. Oil

i.

THE LAST DAY OF ULYSSES REPORTED
BY A SAILOR

He let the oil run over his brow,
down his cheeks and shoulders,
over his hips to his feet where
it was sucked into the howling mountain.
He stood in the dark tent, frail
with victory, the blooded armor on
the dirt, his spear and helmet
lay upon the burlap and golden cloak
he wore in his last attack upon the
savage forms. He broke four vials
of oil into a bowl and breathed in
the sweet green oils like an atmosphere
breathes in the florid rubble of the void.
His body slid upon the air and he
shouted at the pitch vault of the tent
until the wind blew open the tent flap
and he strode out into the raining dark.

His men lay about their dead. Horses
stood in the thunder like tidal waves
and gnawed the wind. From the camp-ground
the half-dead in their doric panic
prepared to storm the slobbering cup-bearer
who lifted up his head above the line of
trees that marked the beginning of the
barricades. The Captain stood upon the
shattered axletree of his wagon, the golden
mountings and jeweled reins hanging in the
bleeding night where the noise of death
hung in the trees, its black plumes and jet
flags blowing on the winds that carried
the waters of the styx upon the spoiled
and upturned olive trees.
                    And in a gesture
that could have been the gesture of a lion
watching the sun spring from the hunter's knife
or an astronomer tracking the final, plundering
star, he turned on the noises and the rains,
upon the horses rocking in the torrents and
walked into the tent where I dressed him in
his armor, handed him his spear, oiled in
the ceremony of death and watched with a sailor's
wonder as he cut a hole in the rear of the tent,
turned upon me, touched my forehead with
his chrismed finger and moved out, silent as a comet.

I do not know the end for I fled
through the camp and hid deep in
the hold of my ship where I stayed

till sunrise. When I woke the day
was bright and in the sky I saw
a glittering heel budge the firmament.

ii.

The wife drops the radish
into the wooden bowl
and the green oils cling to the skin.

The poet spears the word
in the clear streams
and the stones glow like ripe olives.

The child stands his hoop and from
the tree races through it
and the green leaves spin on the olive trees.

The poet stands his self and from
the light leaps over it
and the olives sing in the grinding vats.

The schoolboy walks on the white fence—
and pickets and palings hold him kindly.
And from the olive grove the olive branches
float in their green oils.

Intellectual man casts a line to the
sun-cliff and pulls it tight.
The green-sap tightens in the pit
and the olives suck in the tawny spices of the sun.

Watch the green oils and the olives and the olive groves
when the sun mounts the branches and greenolives,
blackolives, floating in the black alleys
of their leaves, fall into the press that
trundles through the groves pulled by two white
oxen bearing the red signs of fire on their horns.

THE VIRGIN'S HOUSE

This is a well guarded place.
A boy with a bear on a chain
sounds a tambourine in a grove
and lying in the road,
his knees up, a shepherd pipes
on a wooden whistle; below,
the drag of the sea and a line
of camels strung with bells.
These are the watchers who report
all visitors, especially hunters.

Here the air begins to flower
and a cage of hogs, wire-snouted
and toxic in their slime,
have the odor of the heart.
(There is a sanctity that has
no oil and balm but dirt.)
It was here the Virgin came
to wait the dreamer of her womb,
in a grove of bears, on a road of whistles,
where light was stem of the sun.

This is the place called Mary's House,
in Ephesus, where hills mirror the sea
and rocks mirror the earth
and the earth mirrors the precious
minerals of the sun. There was a lady
companioned by a youth with

abandoned eyes and bright memory
who came with chattels and a cat
to rest here: from lights,
from the worshippers.

Place is of the mind; in the stormy
latitudes that cross between the
brain and the graven winds there
are crevices and heights that prepare
for tombs and cataracts the body,
as it moves off like a lamp
into the shafts of space. House
and house's beams and vaults
must repair unto the mind as
images of mountains drive into climbers' rope.

On a day of flint when the hogs
put dents in their wire cage
and the air caught in the cracks like grass,
tambourine and pipe sounded
in the grove and stilled the winds;
bears set up a stamping and a yell
for the Virgin drew her hands
across her eyes when a visitor,
white as broom, in a hunting coat,
lifted the door latch and drew back the bolt.

"I had a dream, I tell you, I had a dream
naked at the rim of hell.
I descried a whirlwind."

I said: "Well enough." Pinned
him with my eyes and asked
how hot it was.

"It singed my palate
I closed my eyes and it
singed my skull-bone.
Out of my mouth I cried."

I said: "Incredible and was it
pestiferous?" (A High Groan)
I set him down before me.
By his hair I brought him
down.

"It glazed my eyelids.
Maggots at my temples;
a heavy dew fell
on my skin. Outrage, I cried."

I said: "No blessing."
"My thighs and belly
burned through; a sulphur
tide gathered at my feet.

'Break, Sham Hot,' I growled
at the diamond wind."

I said: "The assassin pursues.
Sit quiet; lift your feet;
you make the floor smoke."

"All the colors of pain
burned in me; the white
and the black and the red. Aheee
how the jaw-bone cracked
and the neck bent."

I said: "You are deformed."

"When I thought my front-brain
would fall into my mouth,
I heard the sash go up.
The sun ranged on the wall
and I saw you standing on a lake of frost."

I said: "I am Zero."
And closed him four-square round
with ice.

FROM THE WORLD FOUR RAGES CAME

From the world four rages came,
demented marvels of the night,
begotten from the clays of song,
wrested from the veins of God.

The first was earth, the reckoning
force that builds the crystal
in the blood, the line and plane
nonpareil, the mighty chord of ritual.

The next was air, the lymph
that flows through the narrows
of the light, excruciating ether of
astronomies that move the sun.

And fire came, the solvent mix,
the regnant sign and searing
prop, taking up and letting go
the formal, germinal intent.

Then water broke the lucid bone
and made an island of desire,
cornered by the tides and beasts
that hold the world from air and fire.

The rages took my brain aloft
into the center of the sphere
where energy and silence clash
to measure of dark aeons' fit.

When judgment and the wheel
had stopped and skull and heart
rejoined again I saw the light
of earth return, sweet, absolute

and blest, on eagle ruff,
on crater rim, on spine of wit.
This was the place of breaking-up
and my soul exploded like the primal sun.

AS IT WAS THEN IT WILL NOT BE NOW

As it was then it will not be now;
nothing in excess; equilateral;
row upon row of similarities;
equidistant; nothing angular

or bestial. No sound but its
corresponding sound. Every
thing harmonious. Matchless.
The walls unbuttressed; spiders

wove webs paragon; each thing
its place, sunlit, and hard.
But when we lay down naked
and straight, my arms

crossed upon my chest, your
hands resting on my belly,
our heads tilted toward
each other, then, all was patterned

and consentient. But things would
be as they are now and I called
upon your soul and you delivered it
sumptuous and unlimited.

It was then as it never was:
everything in excess and when
the nightbirds perched on the
egg of the sun we leaned upon

our souls and the elements,
first hydrogen and then ice
helium named themselves and all
things were as they never were.

It would be as it never was before
and logos, multifoliate and
winged, chained my genitals
like anchors to the burgeoning suns.

THE GRAVEYARD: RABAT

With my friend I have walked above
the Arab dead and wondered if
the bone and ash we scattered
were the ghosts of some just Arabs
brought to resurrection before their time.

A cliff of clouds had fallen on the air—
taut, massive, heavy in the light,
a stiff vapor that seemed mountains
in my eyes, wandering among the fences
and towers of the dead, to the ancient
rampart on the brink of the Atlantic.

We walked along the sea. I picked
shells; my friend a glaring white-bone
stretched upon his palm, asked me if I
thought a part of some dead Arab had slipped
through the weed and marble of the slope
and slid upon the sand.

(My mind can hold but one thought at most
and then my brain had struggle with a dream,
a grand thing of ancient signs and metaphor,
for a ghost of emerald followed me one day
upon the sea and I could not shake him
from my blood.)
                    "Is this a knuckle
bone?" he said.

Three gulls, their wings
radiant with blaze cracked on the light
above our heads and an Arab, his burnoose
threaded with stems and leaves of sun
fled past us to the Quay and at the edge,
in a stab that nailed the hour to my eyes,
he fell in runs of black and leaden chimes
into the waters at our feet and the bone
we looked at twitched and blasted in the heat.

BEAUTY

1.

He rode long on Beauty's back,
his calves chafing her ribs, the hot
cage of intellect holding her sublime
flints against his blood. Riding along
the strand, in the long sprint to the
perfect poem, along the cutting lights
where Poseidon's water-knife cuts away
the dike from the idiot sea, he
turned on his imaginings and took the course,
clearing the poled air, shaving berries
from the privet, sparking through the
spurred light to mount the posts at the Herculean
jumps that divide the world of mind from
the world of forms, where on each curve
and hurdle of tone, Beauty clanged her
charge, pawed the turf and threw down
the word long locked in the stable of her genesis.

2.

Beauty, undifferentiated, uncaused,
is not one thing all together,
neither the landscape that
courts the ritual of light nor the

sound of water and herbs exploding
at my eyes, nor the black funeral bitch
that paws the coffin lid, but beauty
twisting its way through the sun,
turning the copper, conical towers
of hell and the viper's gills
in the ranging eloquence of style
into alabaster casks where adamant
kindles and gypsum nets smolder
that trap the world like a stone within the mind.

THE BURNING BUSH

This was a caustic bush,
tilled in adamantine earth, shielded
from women and the moon,
locked from the florid current of spring,
branching in darkness, its leaves
falling like chains in the shadows.
It was harrowed by the viper,
who pets his venom under the granite arch.
Camel's dung first fired it.
Bedouin girls, their masks hung with gold,
chimed by it; the gazelle lay
upon it in the night; the ibex wet it
with his tongue. It was
scanned by the lizard and
razed by the sun that clipped
its buds with its scales. It bloomed
in the wind when blood
cracks through the arctic and sends
scarlet gulfs through the light.
It would not burn until mind
conceived its dark genus; it was
no plant to cope with seasons; the brain
its muds and rains and winds
was the burning of the bush. No blackberry,
no herb or specie of rose
could reach its roots to the brain
and thrill the hot vein that
floats on the oils and waxes of the soul.

When Moses came shod with discs
of salt upon a mist
    growing through the sand he stirred
like a spring and from the center
    of the mist a root moved
toward his mouth and from his mind
    a lean branch of flame, pointed
and in the shape of a plow, cut
    the mist and bloomed the burning bush
in the brain of the prophet
    in the Arabian shale. The plant spoke
in a forked tongue, green as a Vegetable God.

THE SHIPBUILDERS AND THE WEAVER

1. The Weaver—Khartoum

The Prisoner, Adam the Weaver,
sits at his circle. His black
fingers shunt one strand of red,
one of yellow toward a pole
that stands at the middle of light.
The world, in the floes of the sun,
rolls on the weave and crostic
of the loom. Hip and thigh
whipped to a totem, Adam the Weaver
threads the stuff and woof of fire,
unscrews the rack and eyes the needle and the flax.

2. The Shipbuilders on the Blue Nile

How the light rises on the keel!
No way like it of the sun; hail
it as prodigy of the tribes
who fall abeam the waters like
black sails and hammer out
an ascension of a keel. Bole
and grain post on the edge
of nails and slip into place
so keel comes up, ringing, from the shore
where the builders, tarred and naked,

breathe in the winds of the Nile
where germens rout in the ruby slit
(the bird of rivers, the flame of rivers)
the joiner, the hasp,
that rises into the breach,
tying in the balance of the vaults
in breadth of cedar and sheen of keel.

I will break my mind with joists,
winches and hammers: damn
poets, painters and music makers.
I'll have BUILDINGS!
               The world
breaks at my drill: saw, nail
and geometric noise fall
low lying fences, thickets and
flowers.
        Ramparts, vaults,
buttresses, piers and ziggurats
center the sun like a capstone
on the land. I say BUILDINGS
to prairies, cliffs, fields of cattle.

The hewn stone plummets, swings
in an arch that grinds the
arena of combat on the grain;
into the slag of bolt and crystal
I drop the sundering wedge
and scaffolds and cupolas
gape like glowworms in the ditch.

Throw your eye on that dome:
see the light scud across the
ellipse, crack on the warrior's
bow and fall on space I've
squared and split. Believe it:
space is a BUILDING and I will build it.

WRITTEN ON THE OCCASION IN CAIRO WHEN A MAN RODE THROUGH HEAVY TRAFFIC ON A BICYCLE CARRYING ON HIS SHOULDER A PANE OF PLATE GLASS FIVE FEET SQUARE

The thing in itself is often not the image
of the thing nor its metaphor. The thing
in itself is perhaps never more than the wrong
way from one particular to the universal of
another sort; from the country where there
are known circumstances to one where there
is the disproportion of all reality. The
fracture of the thing upon its metaphor is
a new violence, a new intermediacy of intellect;
the thing falls out of line and is surprised
in its unconditioned solitude by the metaphor
with its last and perfecting vanity. It is
an election of fires that moves the heart
to its massive, transient laughter.

THE BLACK LADY

Her face leans on my face
and stops the body.
A black cannon bombs the law
and shoots down the fences of the sun.

Her body leans on my body
and stops the blood.
A black sea twists its loins
and pulls upon the surface of the brain.

Her mind leans on my mind
and stops the eyes.
A black moth knocks the light
and lifts the net from the sparking hive.

Her head leans on my head
and cracks the jaw.
A black skull breathes out fire
and burns the drifting waters and the light.

Her loves lean upon my loves
and sails explode.
A black wing cuts the heart
and eagles rush like knives upon my face.

THE TEACHER

(To Jeremiah Durick)

There is a line—I have seen it
between chicory and thistle—
connecting one thing of beauty
with another.
    The leaping arrow
blunts the light, so our minds
press on music in that trajectory
to a point in the air where
the needle of thought pricks
the wall of reason and we stand
like bridegrooms on the verge
of beauty.
    I climbed toward
light through you, a lecherous
target for all music and final
rigors. I loved your hands
and your philosophy; those were
the days when I'd have laid
my life down for your voice and
when I looked up from my book I saw
that I could see through bread and
honey, the long blindness of my
just calamities being suddenly
unloosed and I was free to linger
on the truth, couchant on every
swell of light.

Now my greatest
teacher, dead and closeted away,
your brawn and glory locked in
chains of ash and root, I dream
your hands and your philosophy
in the hours I draw a line
(in the mute talents of my blood)
between one thing of beauty
and another, as the leaping
arrow blunts the light.

A BEAUTY MEDITATES ON BEAUTY

Who knows this ceremony? Beauty guards
my body, paints my blood, is my bone's
joiner, my breath's keep. The earth,
fired and uprooted, brings its syrups
and hot colors to my skin. Chains of
jade, milk, gold and silver, the small
gut of the worm, feathers and pelts
from a wild country hold me, baroque
and spoiling in her barbarous net.
Though I hold my mirror far from the
wind and metal lights, I know that beauty
is the way I'll die—though all men
die with beauty in their arms.

As the chase sends the hunter to seek
the buck torn with lightning on the
cliff and the hound to the mad red fox
chewing up his madness in the pyre
of the oak, so I lie down with beauty
and rise up to feel the deviate lunge
of my spine.
         In the fancy days, I knew
that beauty had no law that doomed
weird girls to dream of toads. Pocked
hearts and those that beauty stuns come
like summer clove and the sweet wild thyme
to bloom and then they crack and are
undone. When I die I pray I'll rot

among the ugly and their kind and when
beauty hacks my soul out of her loathsome
net, in that frigid journey to the pitch
I'll jab the ass of that pale bitch who
laughed me with her dazzle to my grave.

IN HONOR OF THE MOTHER OF GOD

I do not know how I should call her

Pelt
White Door

In a world of toads and electrons
how does man call this drudge of the
ghostly bird

Kite
Wagon
Fish Net

She did not seek
the wedding horn
She formed integral
man who cannonaded on the
wide planked roman light
like wassail
with a sensuous rabbinic gait

He was immaculate as the sea;
his voice cracked with the nap
and rattle of the maelstrom

Loom
Bark
Syrup Bucket

She was the spirit sail
who leaned into the wind
spinning like a green vine

White arrow
Spice of Eden
The Sovereign Wizard of Seed.

STONEGRAVE, YORKSHIRE

Spring, 1963

The Man of the Tribe advances over the
brick walled fields in a casque of hides,
bolted in a pelt ribbed with weeds dried
in the brackish sun. About his waist hangs
a stone hammer; the skins of his shield
are scratched with the names of the first gods.
The taste of intelligence is on his lips
warm as the blood of a goat when its belly
flies open to salty teeth and the smell
of the veins chokes the eyes. He moves
from hillock to hillock, vanishing down
into a valley, up over the crest of a field,
onto a plain, through the wood, snapping
the low branches, tearing up the spring grass,
to the palisades of the Village of Wass
where alarms of burning oil flashed
in his hooded eyes. The law of things
like a drugged light creaked through his
painted brow as ladies of the Hadramaut
beckon to traders in wools and holy parchments
to bring the tack and spoil of play
to halls of grit. He heard the ring
of his voice on the rain, saw the maps of conquest
and took to his mouth the speaking grains:
in the mind's accord all was plenum as he stood
in the axial shadow, in the high summer of signs.

The land rested. The sky atop the brown hills
was buoyant and floated on the light.

To walk toward those hills and to come upon
the clouds at the crest is to remember how
it was to walk on a fence or along a pier out
into the sea; to balance on a log and ride
the waves on a summer current of winds; it is
to swing out from a tree and stretch on the prow
of a dinghy and drag a hand through the waters.
Atop these hills there is no precipice
though it seems chasms fall beyond the walls
where the next field, another hill and sky float,
where the legs stride out upon the earth. Along
the fences sheep graze and in the bronze day, in
the Valley of Wass, the mind knocks against
the heart with green budded staves.

NO WAY NOW BUT SORROW

"But see it from the top,"
he said, "climb with me
to the top and see the small
waves of low water bite the sand."

"Now there is only the mounting sorrow.
Thought takes too much time.
If the suffering will not endure
then I shall surely die;
if it endures I die."

Bartrah Island upon the waters
of the lagoon, a curved space
in the dark. So, too, her mind.

"O come to the top of the island
and look into the ocean.
The waves have raked the sand
into circles; the cockle strand
hisses and purple sea urchin husks lie
on the shingle.
There is no sorrow in the sea."

"Because you know the sea," she said,
"you know of sorrow nothing real.
I feel death come round the top of the island.

It bears the healing part.
The fox and crab measure the shroud.
Death breathes me in."

The Atlantic was still but for the new tide
straining at the sands. She lay upon
the earth and covered the ground about her
with her long black hair that rose
in the breeze and fell across her face
in a black web. Above her, Michael,
her second husband, stood. He said: "Come
with me, I bear the healing part.
Look toward the land, toward our sheep
and the white ponies. The land knows no sorrow."

"Because you're of that land you know
nothing real of sorrow."

She twisted upon the earth and pulled herself
along the edge of the sea. Jammed into the bank,
reared up now at low water, the wreck of the
four-masted Danish schooner, The Sign, rested
on the tidal beach. In the morning the wreck
descended, the sun rose and the sea issued forth
nymphs, fish, iron tide, salt, coral, mailed turtles
and the changeling seals. The fertile waters rode
upon the eye of the reef and through the spiney hops
of the sunburst. The second husband sang the chant
of the Irish morning god, hung cliffs and tides

on the roofbeams of the marriage hut, and bent to his thigh
the sorrowing woman. There was great peace in the town
and the tides mounting into the River Moy rocked
the bells in the channel and the sound of love delivered,
enclosed and puissant, possessed the green isle of Bartrah
that once was dark, tormented and without form.

TO THE MEMORY OF LYDIA HOFFMAN

When she danced upon the counter of his bar in Flatbush
her husband beat her and she came to us bearing
a scar upon her cheek: she limped and wore a flaring
red hat with white flowers on the crown. I was
four months old and she drove me through
the nursery like a whip, oiled my crooked feet with
olive butter and shined my father's hunting boots—
she was in our house like a furnace; she roots

now in my memory with the pikes of her agonies.
She devoured us: we ravaged her, left hoses running
in the gardens and in the afternoon lay drumming
on the attic floor above her room where she rested
after a morning of our barbarities. Lydia wept,
bent over tubs, baited traps and prepared the meals:
we mauled her with cats, muddied shoes and toads:
she studied us as a priest the victims in the sacred grove.

Lydia was born in Zurich in a farmhouse on the river Sihl.
When she was seven the farm caught fire
and burned all day in the white pool of winter. As the pyre
reached to a skin of flame, at the moment the center
timber fell, her father rose up burning on the roof,
black and dumb and threw himself into the air
and fell spinning on the frozen ground:
his neck snapped and he thumped the ice. The sound

of a great wickedness pulled forever at her head
and she dreamed of high flames on mountain tops,
of falling gables and a figure burning in the ruts
of a frozen field. She was queer and hurled dishes
at my father, drank gin with straws and sang the songs
of Heine in the kitchen. Lured by her fury to containment
we learned the dark directives of her mind:
she was broody, lashed and crippled and heard the whine

of thugs in the maple grove, saw poisoned water
in the tap, smelt fire on the stairs. She raged
and cursed, limping through the halls, caged
in her agonies, her brow horned with scales of pain
that spat in the marrow of her legs. But in the spring
when new wheat and cold streams heckle in the field
and animals break down the fences of their pens,
when the field mice and vipers, cocks and hens

yield to the sun, Lydia led us to a hill
where we watched the world break its green egg
as she swung us, hopping in circles, on her game leg.
But as we grew older she grew mad and wandered
in the ice and weeds of winter nights carrying
a lamp to seek a child she dreamed our father
burned and cast into the pool beside the barn
where it lay swelled with toads. Our white farm

house was our priming shed and we were transformed
there into those who knew the ways extremity takes hold.

In her last days, upon a tilted bed, bold
as a withered kore she was baptized and died with
a medal on her nightshirt in the odor of the holy oils.
She lay in her coffin clean as dough, hair in
ringlets, her nails painted red, a peacock power
croaking on the coming lights: from the cool tower

of her rest she calls her father from the chars
of glory. But through the burned shadows and floating
timbers of the mind, Lydia walks, a peg-leg fury, bearing
the sorrow of a great compassion. She stomps her
foot above me, pulls up her sleeves, digs in her
heels and swings the hook and grappling line
to strike the final, mating blow
of first calamities: of the father, the flaming rooftop, the
                                        gaping snows.

I BURN IN A FIRE OF SIGNS

I burn in a fire of signs.
The fireraker and
the walleyed mute shiver on the
drumming jetty
where pentagrams tumble.
On the wide flames of this
dream I sigh in a fire of winds
and sit like a crone by a
pit where a double-jointed fox
rolls on a spasm of black
and lions swim
through waters that hold light still—
as a carved stone holds
a flower still—wind, petal, stem
and blossom; their faces
fix on the branded sea of my dream
and thoughts not mine
rise in the raw clay of my skin
where I wax in this fire of signs
and bear upon my neck the yoke
of heat. A figure of eyes,
its brow etched with
the great, eternal scars
dreams in this fire of signs
where the earth, brute
of my will, bears down upon this
dream, splitting its monumental
crystal plinth, to carry me

aloft into a sky of signs
where the moon clacks.
The sun breathes and an onyx
jaw falls upon this dream
and I am ground in each
sign until the sign
of what I dream becomes
the self I am and each part
becomes the dream: eyes, heart,
spine, liver, phallus: each
is the dream, each the sign,
each the consummation of the dream.